Up SAUCHIE, Doon BUCKIE an' alang ARGYLE

by

Andrew Stuart

D1447595

OVER
100
BEDROOMS
*
*Banqueting &
Conference facilities
for 400*
*
Suites for
DINNER DANCES
TRADE SHOWS
WEDDINGS
LUNCHEONS
*
Ample Parking Space

FOR INFORMATION OR RESERVATIONS
please contact THE GRAND HOTEL, Charing Cross, Glasgow   *Telephone DOUglas 6473*

This publicity card doesn't list the proprietor, but the last one was the United Co-operative Baking Society, the bread makers to many a Glasgow household. Ample parking space in those bygone times meant one could leave the car at the door or around the corner. The day of double yellow lines, parking meters and traffic wardens had yet to dawn. Before digital telephoning, the first three letters of the exchange were required for dialling, followed by the number. A very irate customer once informed the G.P.O. Telephonist that he had been trying for half an hour to obtain a certain Douglas number which had repeatedly given out an unobtainable tone. The operator politely asked what exactly he was dialling. "D-U-G", he replied.

© Andrew Stuart, 1992.
First published in the United Kingdom, 1992,
by Stenlake Publishing Ltd.
Telephone: 01290 551122
www.stenlake.co.uk
ISBN 978 1 84033 665 8

The text has been revised 2014 by Stenlake Publishing with
further information provided by Fergus Sutherland.

The publishers regret that they cannot supply copies of any pictures featured in this book.

The fountain was erected by public subscription to Sir Charles Cameron in recognition of his services to Glasgow during his first twenty one years in Parliament. He was successful with many Private Member Bills, the most notable being the Abolition of Imprisonment for Debt in Scotland. He also sponsored the bill which became the Cremation Act of 1902, making this the legal alternative to burial. Born in Dublin in 1841, he studied medicine at Trinity College with great distinction. He succeeded his father as the editor of the Glasgow-published *North British Daily Mail*, the forerunner of today's *Daily Record*. Sir Charles died in October 1924 and was cremated at the first crematorium in Great Britain, at Woking, Surrey. The fountain is in French Renaissance style. The base is of pink Peterhead granite terracotta Doulton ware mounted on it to a height of 27 feet. There is a bust of Sir Charles, a commemorative plaque, and a clock face at each quarter.

The imposing building on the left is the Grand Hotel erected in 1878, for a time the premier place in town. When the railway companies built their luxurious hotels adjacent to their central terminals, the Grand's popularity declined — the distance being too far out of town for travelling salesmen. This view was photographed circa 1901 and clearly shows that Glasgow was no one horse town. Goods were mainly carried by horse and cart. The carter's life was quite an arduous one, working six days per week, totalling some sixty hours in all. For this he was paid the princely sum of £1:2:0d "Six days shalt thou labour as hard as thou art able, and on the seventh get oot o' bed an' clean the horse and stable." Inevitably, they became unionised and at one time were known as "The Scottish Horse and Motormen Association".

CHARING CROSS, GLASGOW.

A.5921.

This pre-war scene showing the Grand Hotel from Sauchiehall Street would be identical to that seen by most American servicemen from about 1942 onwards. The hotel was taken over by the American Red Cross as their Comforts Club for the U.S. Forces on furlough in Britain. Many wartime romances and marriages were started from the nearby dance halls, including the West End, the Albert, the Berkeley, the Astoria and the most famous of them all, the Locarno! In those days dancing partners were as close as two crisp banknotes stuck together but the present fashion is to be as far apart as bus-stops. The Locarno survived for a time as Tiffany's Disco and thereafter was renamed the Zanzibar Nite Spot, then converted to a casino. The Locarno Club became the "Big Apple" amusement arcade, while the Berkeley became the Highlander's Institute, then later a gaming casino. The Albert and the West End were demolished in the re-development — the sites were rebuilt as part of a new office complex and as a stretch of the M8 motorway respectively.

This partly shows the result of all that upheaval in the early 1970s. Below the landscaped grounds runs the M8 Motorway. In 1968, the Grand Hotel was finally reduced to rubble, and used as infill for the defunct dry dock at Meadowside. Many bemoaned the loss of this well-kent landmark, but now that all the destruction has been tidied up, many agree that the magnificent view of Sir John James Burnet's curvilinear Charing Cross Mansions is sufficient compensation.

Sir John James Burnet (1859–1938), one of Glasgow's most eminent architects, studied at the Ecole des Beaux-Arts in Paris and was influenced by their Hotel de Ville when he designed the Charing Cross Mansions (erected in 1891). He was also responsible for the adjoining Albany Chambers, built in 1897. Both developments were a mix of upmarket apartments and commercial premises. The Grand Hotel, in the foreground, was opened in 1882 and closed in 1968. It was demolished for Junction 18 of the M8 and the exquisitely hideous Fountain House now stands on part of the site. The block in the right foreground also went for the M8 and this is now the site of the even more hideous Tay House.

This postcard dates from just before 1910. The tree is significant as the street's name derives from two old Scottish words, 'sauchie' (pronounced 'suckie') meaning 'willow tree' and 'haugh' (pronounced 'haw') meaning 'marshy meadow'. Unfortunately, someone in the Town Clerk's Office misinterpreted the phonetic haw as ha' (a corruption of 'hall'), thereby causing the misspelling. True Glaswegians always pronounce this as they would Kelvinhaugh Street, Haughburn Road and Flesher's Haugh. The tree is a relic of the many trees that once stood here when this stretch of Sauchiehall Street was occupied by a terrace called Albany Place which was set back from the line of the road and had gardens which are now occupied by Nos. 520 and 522.

That couple passing the three-arched shop would find a great difference in its appearance today. In the early 1990s the premises were partly faced in green marble with gilt lettering and housed the Bank of Pakistan, but this building was demolished sometime after 2010 and in 2014 is a gap site. The gentleman in the foreground might have been studying the prices of musical instruments for this was the warehouse of T.A. Ewing, still standing in 2014, but empty. Above their back entrance is a bust of Ludwig van Beethoven which mystifies many people today in Renfrew Street who are unaware of the former use of the building. The Sauchiehall Street elevation also has two of Glasgow's very own 'Statues of Liberty' (caryatids with some of the same symbolism) as well as the strking 'Harmony' with the pipes and wing, all carved by Glasgow sculptor James Alexander Ewing who also carved the pediment for Glasgow City Chambers which contains the city's most famous 'Statue of Liberty' (actually called 'Truth') and also the angel on the so-called Angel Building on Paisley Road West.

In 1912, the warehouse was converted into the Vitagraph electric picture theatre. During the First World War its name was changed to the King's. This caused consternation among courting couples if their rendezvous was not specified as some would end up at the nearby King's Theatre. When television started the decline in picture-going in the mid 1950s, the cinema became the Newscine — showing newsreels and cartoons. In the early 1960s the cinema became an adult movie club called the Tatler, later the Curzon Classic. It is now a disco named after the guy who started the craze for photographing celebrities in their off-hand moments — 'Joe Paparazzi'.

1892. IN SAUCHIEHALL STREET. GLASGOW.

The flags and bunting are out for the 1938 Empire Exhibition which began on the 3rd of May that year. It was opened by King George VI and held at Bellahouston Park. The Gas Showrooms belonged to the Glasgow Corporation who ran this utility until nationalisation. The shop next to the King's was specially built for T. & R. Annan & Sons, the eminent Victorian and Edwardian photographers and art dealers. Their photographs were used widely on early postcards of the city although they were rarely accredited. This family firm is still in business although now just operates online.

The Regimental Offices of the Royal Highland Fusiliers, at 518 Sauchiehall Street, has a museum on the ground floor. On display here are the uniforms, weapons, pictures, medals and memorabilia of 300 years of the infantry of Glasgow and Ayrshire. The Regiment was the result of the amalgamation, effective from January 1959, of the Highland Light Infantry and the Royal Scots Fusiliers. The new Colours were presented by Princess Margaret, Colonel-in-Chief of the new Regiment, to the Royal Highland Fusiliers at their first ceremonial parade in May 1959. The museum is well worth a visit. In 2006 the regiment was amalgamated with the other regiments of the Scottish Division to become the 2nd Battalion of the Royal Regiment of Scotland. The building which houses the museum was designed by John Keppie and opened in 1904 and connects through to Renfrew Street via an early 19th century house which was another part of Albany Place. The additions and conversion were done for T & R Annan who had their studios there until 1959 when it was taken over by the army.

SAUCHIEHALL STREET, GLASGOW.

Just this side of the Beresford Hotel is 490 Sauchiehall Street, once the Astoria and later the Mayfair Ballroom. This re-opened in October 1987, a year after a disastrous fire gutted it. This venue is now The Garage. Round the back of the Mayfair was another disco, the Venue, where hard rock and reggae music could at one time be heard. Quite a few young bands made their start there including H_2O, Heavy Pettin' and Wet Wet Wet.

BERESFORD HOTEL.
GLASGOW.

William Beresford Inglis was an architect who designed and owned several suburban cinemas including the Arcadia in Calton, the Boulevard in Knightswood, the Imperial in Kinning Park and the Toledo in Muirend. It was his ambition to build a city centre hotel in the Art Deco style. This was achieved when the Beresford, Glasgow's first skyscraper hotel, opened in April, 1938 only a few days ahead of the official opening of the Empire Exhibition. The hotel was designed by his partner, James W. Weddel. Built of reinforced concrete and faced with yellow, red and black tiling, the style was harshly criticized. The comments made included "Another crime committed on Sauchiehall Street", "Custard and Rhubarb Architecture" and "A thing preposterously ugly in both shape and colour — coated in tiles of shrieking red and yellow". Nowadays it is not so unkindly regarded. The hotel's initial year was its most successful, but the outbreak of war diminished the chances to make this enterprise a profitable one and ruined Wm. Beresford Inglis' hotel and cinema empire. For a while it was the Scottish headquarters of ICI and then until 2003 was the Strathclyde University Baird Hall of Residence, before being converted to private flats.

Wm. Lyon was Glasgow's Society Stationer for over a century. Their largest shop premises were at the corner of Sauchiehall Street and Elmbank Street and their printing works were located in nearby Renfrew Street. The windows were full of writing sets, fountain pens, propelling pencils, calendars, visiting cards, postcards and wedding stationery. Their trademark, seen below the clock, was printed on their own local view cards. On the 22nd of October, 1968, in the company's centenary year, a heavily laden builder's lorry came careering down the steep Garnet Street opposite the store and crashed into the shop, killing one woman and injuring 27 people. It took two days to remove the lorry and the dangerous building was immediately demolished, then remained a vacant lot for nineteen years. In 1987 luxury flats and a bank were erected on the site.

This 1933 photograph shows the office premises of David Allen & Sons, who were billposters. The theatrical bills in their front garden are of special interested for in one of the theatres advertised, the Princess's, the title of this book was reputedly first coined in a pantomime. The house and lawn remained as depicted for almost 75 years and had many uses. It was used as a residence, business offices, a dancing studio, a Second World War refugee club, and finally as the rehearsal rooms for the Unity Theatre Players. Standing on this site today is a high concrete and glass building, so uninviting that only those suffering from toothache would dare enter — for this is now the Glasgow Dental Hospital.

326 Sauchiehall Street has been an address renowned for entertainment since October, 1888, when the doors of the Great Scottish National Panorama were opened to the public to view artistic impressions of famous battles. These attractions lasted until 1892, when the premises became an ice skating palace. In 1896, moving pictures were shown to the first paying audience in Glasgow. Hengler's Circus took up residence here in 1902 and remained until 1926, wowing audiences with the antics of Doodles the Clown, the excitement of cowboys and indians and spectacular aquatic finales. The place was then partly demolished and converted into the Waldorf Palais de Danse, but its fate was sealed when Al Jolson started singing to his 'mammy'. Another conversion was ordered and the building re-opened as the Regal Cinema. Al Jolson's second film ("The Singing Fool") was transferred across the water from the Coliseum in 1929 and was an immediate success. The Regal became the ABC, then Cannon, then MGM and then back to being the ABC again. It closed as a cinema in 1999 before being redeveloped as pubs, restaurants and a music venue incorporating the old cinema foyer called the ABC, now the O2 ABC.

Between Dalhousie and Rose Streets is this 1854 building, designed by the architect James Smith. His daughter, Madeleine, is better known for standing trial in Edinburgh in 1858, accused of poisoning her lover with arsenic. A not proven verdict was returned against her. Baillie Archibald McLellan commissioned this project to house his art collection. On his death, the halls and contents were bequeathed to Glasgow Corporation. His estate was insolvent, and, after deliberation, the Corporation paid £29,500 for the halls and £15,000 for the paintings. McLellan's creditors accepted this sum. When the paintings moved to the new art galleries in Kelvingrove in 1902, a group of Glasgow businessmen opened a department store, Treron Et Compagnie, French in name only. The shop went on fire in October 1986 and only the facade survived. For Glasgow's reign as the European City of Culture in 1990, the galleries were completely refurbished to the highest standard for exhibitions, but subsequently leased to Glasgow School of Art for storage.

Miss Kate Cranston, whose tearooms were renowned throughout the city, commissioned Charles Rennie Mackintosh to design the Willow Tearooms in Sauchiehall Street. The work began in 1902 and was completed two years later. It consisted of five separate tearooms, a dining room and a billiards room. The most striking features were in the Room De Luxe tearoom and were considered some of the best examples of Mackintosh's work. In the early 1920s, the tearooms were anglicised to the Kensington, but worse was to follow when they were taken over by Daly's, a fashionable department store, and were much mutilated. However, in 1974, the Room De Luxe was authentically restored and refurnished to Mackintosh's designs. Tea is served upstairs as in Edwardian days — but at today's prices.

Situated between West Campbell Street and Wellington Street stood Sauchie's stores supreme — Pettigrew & Stephen and the competing Copland and Lye. Under the guidance of Andrew Pettigrew, its eventual sole proprietor, Pettigrew & Stephen prospered, extending into Bath Street's Alexandria Hotel and into the Fine Art Institute. Regrettably, this building was destroyed by fire in 1963. The whole block was demolished in the mid 1980s to be replaced by a multi-million pound shopping mall. The only surviving piece was Pettigrew's cupola, designed by Charles Rennie Mackintosh, exhibited at the 1988 Glasgow Garden Festival.

SAUCHIEHALL STREET LOOKING EAST, GLASGOW.

B.8432.

Hugh Fraser acquired many of Glasgow's stores, such as Pettigrew & Stephen, Dallas's, Muirhead's, Henderson's and the big Buchanan Street warehouses for his House of Fraser empire. One day, he walked into Pettigrew & Stephen to hear an assistant say to a customer — "Oh, you'll get it at Lewis's in Argyle Street, Ma'am." He went over to reprimand the assistant and after he had done so, he asked her "What was that customer wanting, anyway?" The assistant looked him straight in the eye, and replied "A number 62 bus, sir."

The loss of Copland & Lye was felt deeply by most Glaswegians who regularly visited Caledonian House. To wander through the large store, pausing to look at fashions, finery and bric-a-brac without the pressures to buy, gave great pleasure to many shoppers. To listen to the strains of "Tea for Two" performed by the musical ensemble in these settings must have been luxury indeed.

COPLAND &
LYE : :

CALEDONIAN
HOUSE,
SAUCHIEHALL
STREET,
GLASGOW.

A CORNER
OF THE
RESTAURANT.

This firm was one of the few establishments not to fall into the hands of Hugh Fraser. By the early 1990s, the owners, the Ogg family, were still trading, albeit in smaller premises, in Milngavie. The old clock, once at the side of Caledonian House, was donated to Milngavie Town Council by Raymond Gillies and now sits at the top of Main Street. It goes periodically (between repairs), bemusing the locals by showing different times on its three faces.

Two of the city centre cinemas were within a stone's throw of each other. In this 1937 view, the one on the left is La Scala and the big feature showing is "After the Thin Man" starring William Powell and Myrna Loy. This was a sophisticated mystery solved by them as Mr and Mrs Nick Castle. As usual, it was their wire haired fox terrier, Asta, that stole the picture. In those days, high teas were served to diners, who could watch the picture at the same time. After the cinema closed down in the late 1970s, the building became another multi-national chain store. Across the road was the Picture House (later known as the Gaumont) and their programme was "Three Smart Girls". This starred Deanna Durbin who became a top box office attraction during the Second World War. The building was once a furnishing warehouse before becoming the Savoy Shopping Centre, under threat of closure in early 2014.

SAUCHIEHALL STREET, GLASGOW.

Further down, at the corner of Hope Street, was another house of fashion, Watt Brothers. Next to this was James Craig's Rhul Restaurant. He had other excellent tearooms throughout the city centre, the most notable being the Gordon. Here, patrons could admire paintings adorning the coffee room walls. Art connoisseurs must have winced at the tobacco smoke damage. Hope Street, by the way, was once called Copenhagen Street, after one of Nelson's sea victories.

Sauchiehall Street, Glasgow

The white building, which the tram car is passing, was the Picture Salon (1914). This cinema did not survive into the era of the "talkies" as it closed down in 1926 and re-opened the following year as Glasgow's only night club, The Piccadilly. The corner of Lumley's was known as Lauder's, named after the original proprietor and not, as the pub sign once suggested, that wee kilted knight with the crooked walking stick Harry Lauder. Outside was the meeting place for theatricals seeking work.

The two thousand seat Royalty Theatre was housed in this building designed by James Thomson and built in 1879–80. The owners Howard & Wyndham, later built the King's and also owned the Alhambra and the Theatre Royal. The Y.M.C.A. renamed the theatre as the Lyrics around 1922 and it was extensively used by amateur dramatic and musical groups. A fire in 1953 caused considerable damage and the building was demolished in 1962. The site was developed as another office and shop complex. The Empire Theatre across the street met the same fate after it closed in 1963. It had survived as Glasgow's music hall from 1874 and was originally called The Gaiety — a sad ending for the graveyard of many an English comedian.

The wheelbarrow in this 1920s view is reminiscent of those laden with second-hand books once stalled in lanes and quiet parts of town for the passer-by to browse through in search of knowledge and bargains. Further down is the canopied entrance to the Buchanan Street subway with its own distinctive aroma, a heady mixture of tar and damp. Opposite this was once the Old Waverley, later the Ivanhoe Temperance Hotel. This bit of the street is now closed to traffic and the underground escalators are in the middle. That unique whiff has also vanished, so smelling salts are no longer required. The church is St. George's Tron of 1807–12, and considered at the time by populace to be too far west of the city centre. In June 2012, the church's congregation seceded from the Church of Scotland over the issue of allowing openly gay clergy and is now based in new premises in Bath Street.

John Burnet designed the Stock Exchange in Gothic style in 1875. His son, Sir John, had extended this the whole length of the south side of St. George's Place by 1906. In an effort to cause embarrassment to the South African Consulate, Glasgow District Council renamed the square Nelson Mandela Place in 1984. The Stock Exchange was completely renovated in 1971 but this, coupled with wear and tear, damaged some of the sculptured works always featured in buildings by the Burnets.

To the left is the former Western Club, built in 1841 to the designs of David Hamilton, now considered the father of Glasgow architecture. The stone was hewn from quarries at Colston, Bishopbriggs. By the early 1990s, The Western Club was vacant and showing signs of neglect. Since 2007 it has been an Apple retail & repair shop. Opposite in this view is a public house belonging to E.H. Cairns. Although long gone now, when it was open, Glasgow's Glaswegian, the late Jack House, wagged that if the Western Club was for businessmen, then the pub should be considered as the Eastern Club for the workers.

Buchanan Street, Glasgow.

St. Vincent Street was the Victorian centre for finance and shipping. That fine building at the left corner is now the Co-operative Bank. It was designed by J.M. Peddie, an Edinburgh man, whose only other building in Glasgow was the nearby Scottish Provident Institution in St. Vincent Place. The ornate lamp standards, cast in local foundries such as the Sun Foundry, have all disappeared from the city.

David Rhind was the architect of the 11-bay Commercial Bank on Gordon Street of 1855. It was extended onto the corner of Buchanan Street in 1887 to a design by Edinburgh architect, Arthur George Mitchell. The Commercial Bank, founded in 1810, was absorbed by the Royal Bank of Scotland in 1969. At the opposite corner is Henry Burton's, a gents outfitter since 1847 which closed in 1997. Only a few shops down is Lizar's, opticians and photographers, who were established in 1835 and were at this address from 1892 until 2006, but are still trading as Black & Lizars.

BUCHANAN STREET LOOKING NORTH, GLASGOW. A.5787

Before the advent of glossy brochures and cheap air fares, Thomas Cook and Sons were the sole travel agency in Glasgow. Shipping firms or their agents dealt directly with customers. Almost opposite was the fashionable men's outfitters, Rowan & Co., famed for stocking the garment no gentleman would be seen without — his belted mackintosh. In the early 1950s, horse traffic was banned from Gordon Street to Argyle Street much to the regret of keen rose growers, but to the relief of office juniors, who were sent out to shovel up the free fertiliser. The premises next to the shops with their sunshades out, were another Kate Cranston tearoom. The internal furnishings were by George Walton with a large mural by Charles Rennie Mackintosh.

Buchanan Street, Glasgow

The arched doorway on the left entered into George Outram & Co's offices, once the publishers of three daily newspapers and numerous magazines and journals. In the morning they published the *Glasgow Herald*, which is now known simply as *The Herald*. They also printed the now defunct *Bulletin*, which was a pictorial daily. From mid-morning till early evening, the *Evening Times* was printed. This is the sole survivor of three local nightly newspapers. After a stay of 112 years here, the Outram Press transferred to premises in Albion Street in 1980, the old *Scottish Daily Express* building. *The Herald* and the *Evening Times* are now owned by Newsquest.

Buchanan Street was named after Andrew Buchanan, who owned the property of four acres from Argyle Street up to Gordon Street. He was the head of Buchanan, Hastie & Co., also of Andrew Buchanan & Co., importers of Virginian Tobacco. The revolt in the colonies caused their failure in 1777 and Buchanan was totally ruined. Most of Buchanan Street is now pedestrianised; it was the first part of the city to become so.

The Argyll Arcade opened in 1828 and from that time onward until the 1960s had a varied selection of shops. Today, most of the shops are jewellers. "Drooko" was the trademark of a successful umbrella manufacturer (couldn't be otherwise with our weather), but perhaps the best remembered and most missed shop would be the Clyde Model Dockyard. Many small boys and grown men had to be dragged away from the windows full of toys and models.

ARGYLE STREET, GLASGOW.

E 0185

The eastern corner of Union Street and Argyle Street has been a popular rendezvous for courting couples for decades, but the newly constructed building of today may not be as inviting as the old Boots' Corner. The department store at the opposite corner in Jamaica Street was Robert Simpson & Co., which later became known as Arnott Simpson Ltd. Argyle Street was named after the 3rd Duke of Argyll, but was once known as the Westergait.

CORNER OF ARGYLE STREET AND JAMAICA STREET, GLASGOW

The Argyle has been replaced by 1932 by the Adelphi Hotel. This was owned by the Dunlop family, who had once been in the theatrical business. Boots' the Chemist let the ground floor shops and, by 1960, they were the sole occupiers. They changed the corner drastically, smothering the facade with blue and cream panelling and adding a large tacky clock. All of this was thankfully demolished in 1989 and a new building put up, a bit 'Mockintoshy', but a great improvement on the last one.

The only recognisable feature in this view is that of the Central Station bridge. Great changes came when the popular Edwardian restaurant, the Queen Anne, burned down in 1951. After looking like a bomb site for a few years, a modern department store was erected on the site. Opened in 1891 under the name Arnott's, it later was amalgamated with its neighbour, Robert Simpson & Sons, to become Arnott-Simpsons, before being renamed Arnott's again. The store was part of the House of Fraser group. Arnott's closed at the end of February 1994 due to the sale of the building, which was to be refurbished for Woolworths, which itself went into administration in November 2008. The Argyle Street store closed in January 2009 after a massive clearance sale in which more or less everything did go, including staff lockers and shop fittings.

Flared trousers and "is it a boy or a girl?" hair cuts suggest this photo dates from around 1970. Freeman Hardy Willis was founded in 1875 and despite several changes of ownership the brand lasted until 1986. Beaverbrooks jewellers was founded in 1919 and are still in business. Embassy cigarettes at this time had almost a quarter of the UK market and its blue coupons were avidly saved up to be exchanged for gifts. By the early 1990s, all four corners were occupied by fast food outlets: McDonald's, Pizza Hut, Dunkin' Donuts & Kentucky Fried Chicken. The first two are still there almost 25 years on and Kentucky Fried Chicken has contracted to KFC.

If you round the corner into St. Enoch Square and look diagonally across to Buchanan Street, the white Art Deco building is occupied by Burton's the Tailors, a Leeds firm. Burton was founded in 1903 by the 18-year-old Montague Burton with a promise to sell high quality suits at low prices. The First World War was a bonanza for the company when it supplied clothing & uniforms for 25% of the armed forces. The inter-war years were a golden age for the firm & by the late 1920s there were 400 shops. During the Second World War, the company once again produced uniforms for the forces. After the war it offered a suit to ex-servicemen which was dubbed 'The Full Monty'. Burton's managed to move with the times despite the loss of its founder in 1952 and still trades today as part of Philip Green's Arcadia Group. At one time, there were many tailors in the city including Claude Alexander, John Collier, Fifty Shilling Tailors, Jackson's, Hector Powe, Weaver to Wearer and West End Misfits.

St Enoch is the corruption of St. Thenaw, the mother of Glasgow's patron Saint Mungo. Both St. Enoch's Square and the Parish Church derive their name from St. Thenaw's Croft, which housed an ancient chapel dedicated to St. Thenaw. The church, built in the eighteenth century, was demolished in the mid 1920s. The toytown-like castle in front of the church was the original subway station. It was designed by James Miller, in 1896, and for a while was Strathclyde Transport's Travel Centre before eventually becoming a coffee shop in 2009. James Miller was also the architect for the 1901 Glasgow International Exhibition at Kelvingrove and posters on the side of the subway station advertise this event.

St. Enoch Station was the main Glasgow terminal of the Glasgow & South Western Railway and was opened by the then Prince of Wales in 1876. The hotel was completed three years later and during the Second World War was the headquarters of Naval Intelligence. Despite an outcry about their demolition, the station was knocked down in 1975 and the hotel demolished two years later. The site was used for many years as a large car park. At one time it was hoped that 8,500 Ministry of Defence jobs would be relocated from London and new offices built on the site. Fans of the TV programme, "Yes, Prime Minister", know that it takes more than a willing government to dislodge our Civil Service from Whitehall.

Laden with luggage, mothers and older children would push prams uphill, while fathers and the young ones would trail behind, all eager to start their holidays at the seaside. In those bygone days, a sunshine holiday was more to be hoped for than expected. Hereby hangs the tale of two Glaswegians who bumped into each other in central Africa. After exchanging niceties about their hometown, one of them suddenly said "You know something, the day's Fair Saturday." The other paused for a moment, looked up at the blazing sun and replied, "An' they're gettin' no' a bad day for it, tae."

BUCHANAN STREET LOOKING NORTH, GLASGOW.

B.634.

The Art Deco kiosk on the left was the Information Bureau for visitors to the 1938 Empire Exhibition and after was the official Tourist Information Bureau until 1956. "Temporary" quarters were then set up in George Square. Thirty years later they moved again to new premises in St. Vincent Place. The Clydesdale Bank corner was once the terminus for Western buses using Renfrewshire routes.1989 saw a great change in the square when the largest glass covered enclosure in Europe opened as the St. Enoch Shopping Centre. The architecture of this building has been criticised, but the interior is bright, clean, warm and, best of all, dry.

114 Argyle Street was an 18th century building which was gifted to Kate Cranston by her bridegroom, Major John Cochrane, in 1892. It was converted into tearooms and became known as the Crown Lunch & Tearooms. George Walton was responsible for the internal designs and the furnishings, all in oak, were by Charles Rennie Mackintosh. Later, in 1905, he transformed the basement into the Dutch Kitchen, with an original fireplace as the room's focal point. The premises were sold in 1917 and most of the decorative work was subsequently covered up. During a renovation, the fireplace and the decorative tiles were discovered intact. A careful photographic record was compiled and the fireplace was subsequently covered up again.

The dome of the massive warehouse and offices at the corner of Argyle Street and Buchanan Street dominates the skyline. Built in 1902–3 for Stewart & McDonald by Horatio Bromhead, the Argyle Street doorway is flanked by two huge sculptured Atlantes. These were immediately nicknamed after the proprietors' surnames. Next to Burton's at the other corner, was Fraser & Arthur's warehouse, which extended into Buchanan Street.

ARGYLE STREET, GLASGOW

This is now the Argyle Street entrance to the St. Enoch Shopping centre. To the west is a twin towered edifice which has survived, despite having a demolition order served on it in 1935. In Edwardian days, it opened as Crouch's Palace of Varieties, then as the Wonderland Theatre. From 1912 until 1935, it was the St. Enoch Picture Theatre.

ARGYLE STREET, LOOKING WEST, GLASGOW.

"As bad as Argyle Street on a Saturday" is the Glaswegian's description of a densely packed area where you have to push to make progress. The crowds flocking to John Anderson's Royal Polytechnic aptly illustrate this. Starting as a drapery store in 1837 in the Gorbals, it progressed into town via Jamaica Street, and was eventually established between Dunlop and Maxwell Streets. Anderson's philosophy was keen prices for a quick return. Later, the "poly" was sold by the founder's son, Sir John Anderson, to Lewis's. By 1935, they had rebuilt on the same site the largest provincial department store in Britain. This record lasted until the 1970s, when the same firm built a larger store in Newcastle-upon-Tyne. In the 1980s, there was a management buy-out, but the National Westminster Bank foreclosed on them and Lewis's went into administration in 1991. The store subsequently re-opened as Debenhams.

John Anderson was one of the pioneers of the department store. He claimed that he had introduced the idea of universal trading under one roof and that this benefited both the shopper and the shopkeeper. The postcard of the Byzantine Smoke Room is so atmospheric that the smell of cigar smoke can be imagined.

The Restaurant Louis XVI

AT JOHN ANDERSON'S *ROYAL POLYTECHNIC LTD* ARGYLE ST. GLASGOW.

As for Milady, the smoke room was matched by the opulence of the rest room adjacent to the Louis XVI restaurant where, amidst luxurious surroundings, a cushion was provided for her tired feet. What a pity that this all ended in the sell-out of 1925.

Argyle Street, Glasgow

The 3d and 6d stores of Woolworth's were plentiful and popular in Glasgow from the 1920s till the 1970s. Their Argyle Street store was the first and largest and there were three others in the city centre. By the 1990s only four branches, in the suburbs, were left in Glasgow. Following the financial crisis in the autumn of 2008 Woolworth's ran out of cash and went into administration later in the year. In January 2009 all Woolworth's shops nationwide closed, although the trading name was sold to an internet retailer. Across from Woolworth's was the Argyle Picture Theatre, converted from a skating rink in 1910. It was one of Glasgow's earliest cinemas and closed its doors for the last time in March 1960. Next to the cinema was Grafton's, a House of Fashion. Their workshop was behind the store and it went on fire in May 1949. Sixteen girls lost their lives.

1929–30 must have been a busy period for construction workers in Argyle Street for Marks & Spencer's stores were put up in this year. These premises were vacated in 1968 when they moved to the opposite corner at Virginia Street. This store was subsequently extended and enlarged. A far cry from the original Mark's Penny Bazaar in Leeds. Across the street was the well-known tailors, Claud Alexander's, and the large brass key, beyond the lamp standard, is on P. & R. Fleming's ironmongery store.

The old Victorian warehouse, which was demolished to make way for Marks & Spencer's, was that of Mann, Byars & Co., who ceased trading in the 1930s. It was once the butt of a schoolboy joke — "Which store in town deals in Slavery?" The answer is "Mann Byar's, of course". In the eighteenth century, the Black Bull Inn stood on this site. A plaque at Argyle Street's intersection with Virginia Street commemorates the fact that Robert Burns stayed here, but it doesn't say with who! During the Second World War, the vacant ground floor was converted into a NAAFI canteen for the Forces. Part of Glassford Street was built on the site of the gardens and mansion of Shawfield. Bonnie Prince Charlie stayed there during the 1745 Jacobite Rebellion.

The building on the right started as the Britannia in 1857. Many Victorian music hall artistes performed here. Friday nights were for amateur turns and audiences would arm themselves with over-ripe fruit to pelt the performers who weren't to their liking. A.E. Pickard re-opened the Britannia and renamed it the Panopticon. This was an amusement complex with waxworks, zoo, museum, moving picture theatre and almost everything else except a circus. There was also a small variety hall and the Friday night amateur slot continued. Stan Laurel and Jack Buchanan made their debuts here. For a time, in the 1920s, the halls became the Tron Cinema, but, in 1927, the name reverted back to the Panopticon. It closed in 1938 and was sold. The ground floor became a shop and the first floor was first used as workshops then as a chicken run. It remained virtually untouched until 1997 when rediscovered by Judith Bowers. It is now managed by a charitable trust and a team of volunteers help it to continue to operate as a living museum of music hall.

TRONGATE, GLASGOW

The steeple on the right is that of Tron St. Mary's. The church was originally the collegiate one of St. Mary & St. Anne which was founded in 1484. This was reconstructed as the Laigh Kirk in 1592. By 1636 the steeple was completed. This was a miniature copy of the Cathedral's central tower. The church was destroyed by fire on the 8th of February 1793 and only the steeple survived. The fourway arches were constructed by John Carrick, City Architect, in 1855.

The reconstructed kirk of 1793 used the steeple from the old church and should have been to the elaborate design of James Adam. During most of this century, it was used by the Corporation's building department. In 1981, it was converted into the Tron Theatre. The equestrian statue is of William of Orange and was presented to the city in 1734 by James MacRae, the Governor of Madras. First erected in front of the Tontine Hotel, the statue was re-sited at the junction depicted. Today, King Billy can be seen near Cathedral Square, being transferred there in 1933. At one time, children sang out "If you want to see King William, take a tramcar to the Cross, there you'll see a noble soldier, riding on a big black horse."

The 18th century Tobacco Lords would be aghast, not only at the crowds walking on their "plainstanes", but that their beloved Tontine Coffee House fronts a massive sign advertising Moore, Taggart & Co. The latter were the local suppliers of uniforms for the Corporation, Fire Brigade, Police and railway companies. Sir John J. Burnet designed the domed, octagonal Glasgow Cross Station for the Glasgow Central Railway in 1896. The cast iron panels which adorned the street can now be found surrounding the public conveniences in St. Vincent Place. Glasgow Cross Station closed down in 1964, but the railway is still in use as part of the Argyle Line.

Mercat Cross, Glasgow.

Most of the tenements behind the railway bridge, both in London Road and Gallowgate, have now gone. St. John James U.F. Church is also gone and only the massive Mercat building remains. Completed in 1928, it looks like a mammoth temple in a Cecil B. de Mille biblical epic. The Mercat Cross, which marked the site of the market, was removed in 1659 and the present one was erected in 1929. It is reputed to be a replica of the original and consists of a balustraded keep, surrounded by a pillar with a unicorn bearing a shield at its peak.